Dialogues on God:
Three Views

Dialogues on God:
Three Views

John L. Hodge
J.D., Ph.D.

John L. Hodge
Publisher

Published in the U.S.A,
by
John L. Hodge, Publisher
P. O. Box 301377
Jamaica Plain, Massachusetts 02130
U.S.A.
JLHPublisher@gmail.com
Your comments are appreciated.
Order books from retailers.

**For more information,
go to the website at
http://johnlhodge.com**

ISBN: 978-0-9831790-2-3

Print on demand services provided by Lightning Source, Inc.

**Printed copies available through
local and online bookstores.**
Check for ebook availability.

CONTENTS

PREFACE

The role of religious faith and the interplay between religion and government affects not only our personal lives but also the politics and culture of nations around the world. These dialogues address many of these complex relationships between personal beliefs and the larger cultural, social and political milieu.

Through a relatively congenial but frank interchange among three siblings, the dialogues highlight three very different ways of living and apprehending the universe. One sibling has a traditional view of God (traditional, that is, within a Christian/Judaic/Islamic context). One has a very different view of God. And one is an atheist. Their interchange reveals interconnections between their views about God and about politics, society, beauty, science, personal relationships, individuality, good and evil, and war and peace.

Of course, there are more than three views about God. This interchange among the three illustrates how very different and conflicting views about God impact their views of practically everything else.

But how can those with such conflicting views live together in the same community, the same society, the same world?

By challenging each other in eleven dialogues, the siblings, in spite of their conflicting views, come to a common realization and agreement. To find out what it is and to understand how they get there, read the entire text of the chapters that follow.

ACKNOWLEDGMENTS

Although the final text is fully my responsibility, I thank Barbara Beckwith, James Reed, and my wife, Diane Franklin, for their comments on previous drafts.

One

HARRIET: I'm glad we could get together after all of these years.

MARTIN: We're family, brothers and sister. We should get together more often.

BOB: I don't know. There are too many arguments in our family, even among us. It's not always pleasant. When I have time to go on a vacation, I'd rather be with my wife and child or with friends than with our own parents. But it is good that the three of us can get away for a walk, especially in this lovely park.

HARRIET: This place is so beautiful in May. Only two months ago it was cold, brown and the trees were barren. Now it's lush, green and full of colorful flowers. Those azaleas are so intense. Our parents are so lucky to live nearby. This is a wonderful resource.

MARTIN: This is God's creation. It's beautiful because God made it so.

BOB: What's God got to do with it? Just enjoy it. It doesn't matter how it got here.

MARTIN: You have no curiosity. If you're curious, you

want to know how things got here. Only God can create such beauty.

BOB: So what about the gloomy, cold winter we just had. Did God create that too?

MARTIN: How can you enjoy the spring if there is no winter? It's all a part of God's plan.

HARRIET: Oh you guys, quit arguing. Let's just enjoy the walk.

MARTIN: Plain beauty by itself is empty, without meaning. It must be connected to something meaningful.

HARRIET: Sorry Mart, that makes no sense to me.

BOB: Well, I can enjoy the beauty and also think about it. I think beauty evolved over many millennia. The flowers became beautiful to attract the bees so the bees could carry pollen to other flowers so the flowers can reproduce. The ugly flowers died out, perhaps because the bees didn't like them. I know that that doesn't explain much, but I wonder about it. Maybe spring is beautiful to inspire animals to feel joy that inspires them to mate.

MARTIN: You reduce our sense of beauty to that of insects!

BOB: Well, it's just a conjecture. I wouldn't be surprised, though, if the beauty bees see is similar to ours. After all, we both like honey. Science still has a long way to go to explain our sense of beauty, but some day we'll figure this out.

HARRIET: It doesn't need explaining.

BOB: I agree that beauty doesn't need to be explained to be enjoyed, but, like Mart said, when you are curious you want to explain these things even if you don't need to. You can enjoy the view and explain it too.

Only God can create such beauty. (Martin)

MARTIN: It doesn't matter what science says about beauty. These lovely trees, these beautiful flowers, you and me—it is impossible to conceive how these things could be created without God. It takes a higher intelligence to bring these things into being. We human beings with our diminutive minds could never create such things. We cannot create life. Only God could do that. Those who question God's existence need only to look around them to see the marvel of life and the complex variety of living things. This cannot be explained without God.

BOB: I agree that there is mystery about life, nature and beauty that we cannot explain, at least not yet. But this mystery and the awesomeness of life is something we can accept and live with without attributing it to an unseen thing called "God." Besides, once you attribute the creation to God, you are still left with the big question of where did God come from. Did God create Himself? Is there another God who created God, and another God who created that God, and so on? I don't see a need to postulate God, because saying God created it just raises more questions.

MARTIN: God is not a postulate. God is! When you believe in God, there is no reason to ask those questions about where did God come from. That's foolish. God is God. God is our creator and the creator of all things.

BOB: But as a scientist, I do not postulate things that aren't necessary to explain things. Nature has evolved over many millennia, and the way things are today are the result of that evolution. I don't need God to create it. God is an unnecessary postulate.

God is an unnecessary postulate. (Bob)

MARTIN: Isn't evolution a postulate?

BOB: It was just a postulate at one time. But it is not just a postulate anymore, because evidence gathered, first by Darwin and examined and confirmed many times since has supported it.

MARTIN: So are you saying that evolution is a proven fact?

BOB: No, a scientific theory, no matter how much evidence supports it, is not the same thing as a fact. There is more to the world than just facts and conjecture. Facts are directly observable things. Theories can be supported by facts or refuted by them. Evolution is a fully supported theory, supported by observable facts.

MARTIN: You scientists are always looking for some way to keep God out of it. Can't you be a scientist and believe in God too?

BOB: Many do, but I think believing in God gets in the way of human progress. Saying that God did it is lazy. We scientists want to explain everything based on what we can observe. No diseases would be cured if we threw up our hands and said you are sick because God did it. By not believing that God did it, we were forced to inquire about the causes of diseases, and we've come a long way. Increasingly I think belief in God is harmful to progress.

MARTIN: I'm not saying that scientists shouldn't try to treat diseases. But really, what progress has science made? You find a treatment for one disease and a new disease crops up. You can't get rid of disease. Disease is part of God's plan. We do not understand His plan, and disease causes suffering, but suffering is also part of God's plan. In some ways science has made matters worse. You create an antibiotic and the disease bacteria become resistant. Now it looks like the bacteria have outsmarted the scientists. There are bacteria now that medicine cannot kill. So as science tries to cure diseases, science makes new diseases possible by creating drugs that cause resistant bacteria. God made smart bacteria and there is not much science can do about it.

HARRIET: I don't agree with your argument, Mart. Science did not cause bacteria to become resistant. You have to look at the matter more carefully. Scientists developed antibiotics to kill bacteria that cause disease. Doctors administered the antibiotics to patients with instructions to take them for so many days. Many patients did not follow the instructions and stop taking them too soon, which allowed some of the bacteria to remain alive and develop resistance. It's not all the patients' fault, since a lot of times doctors, many of whom are not trained as scientists, prescribed antibiotics when they were not needed. Drug companies that made the antibiotics encouraged their use so they could sell more drugs. The failure was not the scientists who developed the antibiotics but what happened after the antibiotics left the laboratory. The problems were not caused by scientists but by, but by, ah, just a lot of things went wrong and still go wrong. So I don't think science is the problem. We need more of it, not less.

BOB: Spoken like a true scientist, Harriet. Why didn't you go into science?

MARTIN: But it doesn't matter what science does. If God wanted there to be no disease, there would be no disease.

BOB: I agree with Harriet. We have to keep studying what goes wrong and fix it. We make mistakes and learn from them. It seems to me that your so-called "God" would not have created humans to be scientists if "He" did not want them.

MARTIN: What do you mean, "so-called God"? You deny that God exists!

HARRIET: OK guys, calm down. We don't all agree, so let's just accept that and not get into a fight.

MARTIN: The problem with you scientists is that you think everything is bits of matter moving around meaninglessly, without purpose. That means we are meaningless and without purpose. That means the beauty around us is illusory.

BOB: When some scientists say that we are nothing but bits of matter moving in accordance natural laws, they are not speaking as scientists but as speculative philosophers. There is no way science can prove the nonexistence of what it does not study. Just because it studies the motions of matter and energy does not mean that that's all there is. There's a lot we don't know, and rather than saying that what we don't know does not exist, I think we should just acknowledge that there is a lot we don't know yet and maybe some day we'll find out.

MARTIN: So you are saying that science cannot prove that God does not exist?

BOB: Right. God is not something science tries to study, so science cannot know anything about God. But that does not mean that God exists. I have no reason to believe in God. To me, God is just an unverified postulate and believing in God does more harm than good.

MARTIN: So how do you find purpose in living if there is no God?

BOB: I enjoy living. I enjoy the quest for knowledge. I enjoy the beauty of this park. I love my wife and my child. I don't need God to have a reason to live.

MARTIN: That's very hedonistic.

BOB: I don't have a problem with it.

MARTIN: Harriet, are you an atheist too?

HARRIET: No, but I don't think of God the way you do.

MARTIN: But you do believe in God?

HARRIET: I'm not sure what I call "God" is what you'd call "God." I can't explain it now. You know, it's getting to be dinner time. I think we need to head back and think about other things. Do you want to get some drinks and snacks?

BOB: Back to our parents and more arguments with them. Oh well, I guess I can deal with it for a few days. My wife is off with her parents having the same problem I am here, so we'll have a lot of commiserating to do when we get back together.

HARRIET: Oh, it's not that bad. Let's enjoy the food, at least. They go to bed early, so we can continue our discussion later.

I'm not sure what I call "God" is what you'd call "God."
(Harriet)

Two

BOB: Well, the evening wasn't so bad. Now that they've gone to bed, we can enjoy the rest of the evening here in the living room and enjoy our cordials. I'm glad we didn't have any big arguments with our parents.

HARRIET: That's because we avoided talking about politics, religion, global warming, alternative medicine and family values.

BOB: Right. Boring.

MARTIN: But if you don't have disagreements and arguments, you never expand your horizons.

BOB: Their horizons end with the back yard.

MARTIN: Speaking of disagreements, Harriet, you said you believed in God but you wouldn't explain. Could you explain?

BOB: Yeah, I'm curious too.

HARRIET: My problem is that I have not figured it all out. My views are fuzzy and hard to articulate. I'm not even sure that what I believe in should be called "God," but there's something going on that suggests a source of energy that science cannot account for. Love, for example. I don't think love is just a chemical reaction to the way someone smells.

Love goes beyond sexual desire and connects us to people we never met, let alone smell. If I see a picture of a crying mother who has lost her child, I want to comfort her in some way. It doesn't matter if the mother is Asian, African, white, green or purple. If I learn that the child was killed by someone, I get angry at the killer and want the killer captured. If I hear that someone in China or Syria or even in the United States has been jailed or attacked because of his or her political or religious beliefs, I get angry. If I see people revolting against an oppressive government, I want to support them. If people are homeless because of an earthquake, tsunami, or hurricane, I want to help them recover and get back to their normal lives, and I nearly cry when I see their homes and communities destroyed. I don't understand what these feelings are about. Why do I have them? Why do I care? Why can't I just focus on my own life and pay no attention to these other people who suffer? There is some kind of energy at work here that I cannot explain. I think of it as the energy of God within us. So that's what it's about for me.

MARTIN: God is only within us if you believe in God. What you are talking about is not God Himself but something else. You sound like you want to support everybody and anybody, but you have to make judgments about people and support those who believe and not be so indiscriminate. Those who do not believe do not deserve support. You are letting your feelings dominate you without being discriminate. You have to distinguish those who believe from those who don't.

> There's something going on that suggests a source of energy that science cannot account for. (Harriet)

HARRIET: My feeling of caring for people does not depend on what they believe. When I want to help someone, I don't care what they believe? You know, an old friend, who's black, told me that many years ago he helped an older white woman who had fallen down. He said that same woman might call him a "nigger" the next day, but he wanted to help her anyway and did. I told him that he did the right thing, and maybe she'd remember that he'd helped her and begin to think differently, but that's not why he helped her. He helped her because she had fallen down and needed help. He probably should not have assumed that she was a racist just because she was white and old, even though it was many years ago, but the point is that he was going to help her even if she was a racist. That's the kind of thing I am talking about. When I see someone is suffering, I want to help and don't care what that person thinks or believes. That's the way I am, and I wish others were like that too. In fact, most people I know are like that.

MARTIN: I'm not so generous as that. I don't think I could help someone who hated me. Would you help someone who was a terrorist?

HARRIET: How am I supposed to know who's a terrorist?

BOB: Well you take out your smartphone, take a photo and use your app that connects to Homeland Security's photo identification service. Just kidding—ah, maybe.

MARTIN: OK, you may not know. But my point is that not everyone deserves to be helped. If I knew the person was my enemy, I would not help him.

HARRIET: If the person was a criminal on the loose, I'd want him captured. But if he was starving, I'd give him food if I could without endangering myself, or if he'd broken his leg,

I'd call for help. It's the humane thing to do. It wouldn't matter that he is a criminal. Still, I'd want him to be captured and brought to trial, so I'd call the police as well as an ambulance.

MARTIN: Why is it humane to help a criminal? See, something's not right about your idea of God. What you are calling God doesn't know the difference between good and evil. God doesn't exist within people. God stands outside of us as our creator. God helps good people and imposes suffering on bad people. When you help bad people, you contribute to evil. So what you are calling God isn't God at all.

HARRIET: Well, it's what I call God, or God-energy, or something like that. It's what I experience. What you call God is something I don't experience. It's too conceptual. Like Bob said yesterday, God is a postulate, an idea, not something you directly experience. So I guess that means I don't believe in God the way you think of God.

MARTIN: Right, you don't believe in God. Essentially you are an atheist like Bob. What you call God is not God.

BOB: I don't think Harriet is an atheist. She just thinks about God differently from you.

MARTIN: Look, God is the Creator of the universe. Her so-called God doesn't create anything. What she calls God is just a bunch of feelings. God knows the difference between good and evil. Her God doesn't. Believing in God is a matter of faith, not just a bunch of feelings. When you have faith in God, you experience God, and you know the difference between good and evil. When you don't believe, you don't know the difference. What she calls God doesn't know the difference, so what she calls God is not God.

HARRIET: I know the difference between what's good and

what's bad. What's bad is not to help people who need help, if you are able to do it. What's bad is to harm someone else for your own benefit. You say that what I'm calling God is not a creator, but that's not true. The caring and loving energy I experience in myself and in others is the energy that motivates me to work towards improving the lives of others. That energy creates my day and makes my life worth living.

MARTIN: You sound like a saint.

HARRIET: No, it's not about being a saint. I enjoy what I do. I enjoy helping others, and I know I have to help myself be strong and healthy so I can help others. I think of saints as engaging in self-sacrifice to help others. I don't believe in self-sacrifice. I do what I do because I enjoy it. It's not self-sacrifice or duty; it's self-fulfillment.

MARTIN: That's really confused. When you believe in God, you are willing to sacrifice for God. Being good is not about self-fulfillment. It's about doing God's will.

HARRIET: But self-fulfillment is not about being selfish, not the way I see it. You are helping others live more fulfilling lives, more fulfilling to them. Doing that is fulfilling to me. So my self-fulfillment and that of others are all part of the same thing. I enjoy helping others live more fulfilling lives, and that is fulfilling to me.

MARTIN: See, for you it's all about enjoyment and fulfillment. I think that's selfish. When you believe in God, you do God's will and it doesn't matter whether it brings you pleasure. Doing God's will requires self-sacrifice. If you do only what feels good to you, you are ignoring what God wills.

BOB: You guys are going around in circles. You are never going to agree. I'm going to bed and get some sleep so I can enjoy tomorrow.

HARRIET: You know, this discussion has helped me think things through. I've never said before what I said today. I think I'm beginning to understand myself a little better. But I agree with Bob—it's bedtime.

When you believe in God, you do God's will and it doesn't matter whether it brings you pleasure. (Martin)

Three

MARTIN: What a beautiful cloudless morning. There's another path in this park I'd like to take. Is that OK with you?

BOB: Fine with me.

HARRIET: Me too.

MARTIN: Harriet, how is your son doing?

HARRIET: Oh, he's fine. He's quite a young man now, going to be a sophomore in college this fall. He's still not quite sure which way to go, into political science or mathematics.

MARTIN: At least with mathematics he might find a job. What would he do with political science?

HARRIET: Well, he's interested in government, in human rights, in international law. I think he's more interested in that than in math, though he seems good at math. I think he should pursue what he wants.

MARTIN: What's the point of having a degree if there's no jobs for you? He should stick with math. Don't you think so, Bob?

BOB: I don't think you can predict today what jobs will be available by the time he graduates. Or ten or twenty years after that. I'm in favor of pursuing what interests you. What's the point of spending your life doing something you hate just to earn money?

MARTIN: What's the point of learning a lot of stuff, getting a bunch of degrees and ending up in the unemployment line looking for a handout?

BOB: Well, you could end up unemployed no matter what you study for. The jobs available today may not be around tomorrow. Thinking of college as just a way to get a job is short-sighted. With a broad education you can get the tools to be flexible and pursue your own interests at the same time.

MARTIN: Sure, if you don't starve first.

HARRIET: I want to be in a society where starving is not a problem, where people support one another and make sure others have enough to eat. Those who have jobs should share with those who don't, at least enough so everyone has enough to eat and a place to stay.

MARTIN: If you believe in God, you don't have to worry about those things. God will take care of you.

HARRIET: I think we should take care of each other.

MARTIN: But you would feed those who are evil as well as those who are good, those who believe and those who don't.

HARRIET: I'm not sure I believe in evil.

MARTIN: That's because you don't believe in God. Without believing in God, you can't know right from wrong.

BOB: So how do you know right from wrong?

MARTIN: You seek guidance from God. For one thing, you distinguish those who have faith from those who don't.

BOB: I don't understand faith. It makes no sense to me.

I'm not sure I believe in evil. (Harriet)

MARTIN: You have faith in science. Harriet has faith in people. I have faith in God.

BOB: No, I don't have faith in science. It's not about faith, it's about experience and probability. Science studies things that happen, things that people experience or can experience and uses that experience to confirm or question ideas or theories. Confirmed theories help us predict what will happen next, not with absolute certainty but with probability. Look at medicine, for example. If I get an infection, a doctor will prescribe a particular medicine that has been tested and will be likely to cure the infection. I don't take the medicine on faith, I take it because I know that studies have shown a high probability that the medicine will help. If I have reason to doubt the doctor, I'll look up the medicine on the internet and research it. Actually, I'd do that anyway to know what side effects to look for. So I don't even have faith in the doctor. I research the medicines prescribed for me and will question the doctor if I think another medicine might be better or cheaper and just as good. I don't see any place for faith here. It's about experience and learning about the experiences of others.

MARTIN: All of that experience is about the past. None of it will guarantee that the sun will rise tomorrow. You can't prove it will. Just because it has done so in the past does not mean it will in the future.

BOB: But I don't need faith to say the sun will rise tomorrow. I know about the motions of the planets and stars like our sun. I know the laws of physics. I know that based on

---

I don't understand faith. It makes no sense to me. (Bob)

what we know, it is reasonable to predict that the sun will rise tomorrow.

MARTIN: But those laws might be wrong. You can't prove they are right or won't change tomorrow.

BOB: That's true, but I don't need faith to guarantee that the laws are right. All I need is enough assurance based on what I know to plan for tomorrow. If I'm wrong, I'm wrong and so be it. But it makes more sense to assume that the sun will rise tomorrow than not. If it does, I have prepared for it. If it doesn't, then it won't matter anyway, because we'll all be in the same pickle and have to figure something out that's new, if we are alive at all. So it's not about faith but about what makes sense based on what we know.

MARTIN: I think my faith is superior to your science. With faith, I can know that tomorrow will come, even if I am not alive tomorrow. God provides the guarantee. You cannot have a guarantee without faith in God.

BOB: I don't need a guarantee, just a good probability. I just don't understand faith.

MARTIN: Faith in God is an absolute commitment to do God's will. It's a spiritual thing. It is something you do without question. It is a complete giving of yourself to God. You've heard of the story of Abraham and Isaac? It shows you what faith means. It means, like Abraham, you would kill your only son if God commanded it. That he didn't actually have to do so is beside the point. He was going to do it, because God commanded it. Faith in God means that God's will and your connection to God are more important than

---

I think my faith is superior to your science. (Martin)

anything in the world.

HARRIET: Frankly, Mart, I think that story is the most disgusting thing I've ever heard. A God that commands that I kill my child is not a God I believe in. My connection to my child is one of the most beautiful and precious things on earth, and if I thought God asked me to kill him, I'd conclude I was ready for the mental hospital. The other thing that bugs me about that story is that God asked Abraham and neither Abraham nor God asked Sarah. It's a story that puts men above women, the male above the female. God is male, Abraham is male, Isaac is male. Sarah the mother is irrelevant. Who cares what she thinks? If God had asked her, she might have told God to go to hell. If Isaac had been a girl, Abraham would not have been anguished about it and said, "Sure God, no problem." I hate that story.

BOB: That story is one of the reasons I don't believe in God and why I think belief in God is a bad thing. How many murderers are there who think they are another Abraham following the will of God? Lots. They are delusional and crazy. Their belief in God feeds their delusions and craziness. Every tyrant I know of, including some of our presidents, justify killing others by thinking God is on their side. We'd all be better off if God was not in the picture.

MARTIN: You are both taking it too literally. It's just a story to explain the meaning of faith. It was written at a time when men were in charge. The same story could be told today with women. A mother who would have done as Abraham did would show the strength of her faith.

BOB: I think some mothers have in fact killed their children thinking that they were commanded by God like Abraham. They were guilty of murder. They were also crazy, so maybe some of them were not guilty due to insanity. Either way, such faith is dumb and we would be better off without it.

HARRIET: Actually, I think God is present in my connection to my son. It's awesome. So obviously God, as I see it, would never ask me to kill my son, for God would be killing a part of God. Your God, Mart, stands totally outside of my connection to my son and judges from above. That's why I think of God differently from you.

MARTIN: It is so hard for a believer to explain faith to nonbelievers. I can see that you both are well defended against faith and nothing I say will change your minds. You are closed to faith and I can't open you up to it.

BOB: Every time I try to understand faith it makes no sense to me. I think once you commit to faith, you close off to any alternative. Experience no longer has any say.

HARRIET: I am not clear on the difference between faith and trust. I trust my son to make the right decisions about his life. When I drive, I trust other drivers headed in the opposite direction not to swerve in front of me. When I send an email, I trust the internet to deliver the message or send me a bounce. When I buy something in a jar, I trust that what's in the jar is what it says on the label. It seems like almost everything I do in life requires me to trust someone or something else. I can't verify everything, so I trust others to do what they should. Is this faith? Actually, I don't think so. My trust is something I presume, like saying I trust you until you give me a reason not to trust you.

> A God that commands that I kill my child is not a God I believe in. (Harriet)

BOB: I think of trust as like a working hypothesis that can be verified or not. In some situations the trust is not verified, or is contradicted by experience, so my trust in that is broken. I trust until experience refutes the hypothesis in that particular instance. But I continue to trust until I experience something that calls the trust into question.

HARRIET: But why do you hypothesize trust in the first place? Is it faith that leads us to trust?

BOB: I think it's just how we evolved. If you don't hypothesize trust, you become immobile, because, like you said, you can't verify everything. If you do try to verify everything, life becomes impossible. As we evolved, people who didn't hypothesize trust died out, because they couldn't function.

HARRIET: I know someone like that who is paranoid about everything. She trusts no one. She can't function. She's a basket case. So maybe trust is just something we have to do to live, and if we want to live, we find it necessary to trust. So I do see this as different from faith. Once you commit to faith, I'm not sure there is any experience that can change it. But trust can be broken by experiencing someone who can't be trusted. You break the trust with that person but keep the trust for others. You have to just to function.

BOB: I think faith in God, once committed to, can't be broken no matter what happens. Experience becomes irrelevant. For me, anything that can't be verified or refuted by experience should be ignored.

> Faith is a spiritual thing, not something that is rational to our little minds. (Martin)

MARTIN: You have to understand that faith is not rational. Faith is spiritual. Spirituality is superior to rationality. To you, rationality is superior to faith and earthly things are superior to God. But rationality is just a human way of thinking. There is no spirituality in it. God is greater than anything human. When you have faith in God, you recognize that human rationality is just a barrier to God.

BOB: To me, rationality and experience is all we have. I'm sticking with it.

HARRIET: Maybe we define rationality and experience too narrowly. I experience things that I cannot explain. I experience energy between people, laughing together, dancing, music, love, that I cannot explain rationally. I think there is a good energy that binds us together and makes us human. It's like there is God within us, in all of us, that is this energy or the source of it. Sorry, Mart, I don't think this energy has anything to do with your faith in God.

MARTIN: Your beliefs, Harriet, root you to the physical earth. God is spiritual, not earthly. Faith is a spiritual thing, not something that is rational to our little minds, and it is not of the earth. Your connection to your son is an earthly thing, not a spiritual one, just as the sex that got you pregnant was a physical thing.

HARRIET: Your view is that spirituality is separate from the body. My view is that spirituality resides within our bodies. To me, my connection to my son is a connection of the Godliness within me to the Godliness within him. The same kind of connection happened during the love-making that

---

Spirituality resides within our bodies. (Harriet)

produced my son. My late husband and I merged our Godliness together into some joyous moments. Those ecstatic moments were both spiritual and physical. We felt joined together into something beyond either of us separately.

MARTIN: So you were having sex with God? That's disgusting!

HARRIET: No, it's wonderful. You see, God is within us, not up in the sky.

BOB: I agree that sex can be wonderful. But it's the beauty of two bodies enjoying each other. Our lovely bodies have evolved to be what they are as a part of nature. I see no reason to bring God into it.

HARRIET: I think if people believed God was within all of us, there would be no rape or sexual abuse. We'd see sex as a precious thing involving the lovers as whole persons and not merely a means for one's own pleasure. The other's body would be seen as the home of that person's spirituality, of that person's Godliness within.

MARTIN: You both are very earth bound. Spirituality is missing. Spirituality is not a physical thing. Sex has nothing to do with it.

HARRIET: To me spirituality and our bodies cannot be separated. Making love is both physical and spiritual.

BOB: I don't think there is any such thing as spirituality. Just because science doesn't know something does not make the unknown spiritual. But speaking of being earthbound, my legs are tired and my stomach is growling. Let's go get some lunch.

I don't think there is any such thing as spirituality. (Bob)

Four

HARRIET: I love this outdoor café. We can eat and hang around afterwards as long as we like. No one bugs you to leave.

BOB: This is great. I wish more places were like this.

MARTIN: Most places can't afford to rent space without selling something.

BOB: So Mart, one thing you said really bothers me. You said faith is above reason, or rationality. I don't get that at all. It seems to me that without rationality, you go crazy. You need rationality to make sense of things. Surely you must have a reason for having faith.

MARTIN: You need faith to commit to God. Rationality gets in the way. Reason is a barrier to God.

BOB: But that's circular. You need faith to commit to God, because rationality is in the way, and rationality is inferior to faith because rationality prevents you from committing to God. You are going around in circles. What if rationality is not inferior to faith? What if it's superior.

MARTIN: Circularity is a rational concept. Yes, when you have faith you leap into a higher spiritual realm where circularity is not a problem. Besides, you are being circular when you say that rationality is good, because it's better than faith. How do you prove that? The only way you can prove that rationality is better than faith is by being rational. So you are in a circle too, except that your circle of rationality rejects circularity, so to be fully rational you should reject rationality.

BOB: You misunderstand rationality. Rationality is scientific in that it is a process that connects concepts and ideas to experience. The whole idea of rationality, if it is scientific instead of Cartesian, is to connect thought with experience. That keeps the mental process within us connected to the world that is outside of us. It's that connection that prevents circularity.

MARTIN: But what makes you think that your scientific rationality, or whatever you call it, is any better than faith?

BOB: Because faith disconnects you from experience. Once you commit to faith, experience no longer matters.

MARTIN: No, faith connects me to the experience of God. Your rationality will not allow that.

BOB: I'm not sure you are experiencing anything but an illusion.

MARTIN: And since you have no faith, you will never know. It can't be an illusion, because all over the world and throughout history, most people believe in God or in some spiritual realm beyond the physical realm of experience. All these millions and billions of people can't be believing in an illusion.

BOB: I'm not so sure. You say rationality gets in the way of faith; I say faith gets in the way of rationality. History is full of masses of people believing in illusions. Before science most people believed the world was flat. That was wrong. The medieval priests proved that the sun revolved around the earth and later refused to look in Galileo's telescope. They all believed in an illusion. Before people believed in one God, they believed in all kinds of different spirits and gods. And among those who believe in one God, they are divided up into different religions and sects, and they all believe something different. They cannot all be right. I think the difference between science and all these unscientific beliefs is that science aids the growth of humanity, whereas all these different religious sects often end up fighting one another and killing one another. They contribute to the decline of humanity, not to its advancement. I think the wars they have with one another is the experience that proves that they are believing in illusions, dangerous illusions. Science does not lead to war. When scientists disagree among themselves, they do more studies to get more experience to find the right answer or the best hypothesis. It's a peaceful process of settling disputes. I think it's wonderful.

MARTIN: My experience of God is wonderful, and that's why I believe in God. You see, there actually is a reason for having faith. It's to preserve our individuality. My primary relationship is between me and God. Through my faith I know I am unique, that God loves me. By being guided by God, I am not drawn into doing what everybody else does. I don't get lost in a crowd, or have to have the latest fashions, or have to agree with anyone else. God affirms my existence, so I don't need others to do it for me. When faith falters, people

> You say rationality gets in the way of faith; I say faith gets in the way of rationality. (Bob)

become too dependent on the approval of others, they merge into the masses and get lost. God gives me the guidance to steer my own course.

BOB: Seems to me that believing in God is to join the masses and get the approval of others who also believe in God.

MARTIN: That happens when faith falters, as is the case with most people who say they believe. They believe because others believe. That's not true faith. True faith is between me and God, and what others think or say does not matter.

BOB: Maybe. But scientists are also individuals, whether they believe in God or not. Each one pursues his or her own experiment or study to advance knowledge. Anyone with a well-documented experiment can challenge the conclusions of others. But the individual does not get lost in his or her own illusions, because knowledge depends not just on one experiment but requires that other scientists are persuaded, so there is a check on the individual who gets so caught up in his own way of thinking that he can't see his own errors. So the scientific community both preserves individuality and connects the individual to a broader community. The individual does not get lost. I think it's hard for an individual who looks to God for direction to know whether he's directed by God or directed by an illusion. In science, the individual is called upon to persuade others to advance knowledge, so the individual neither gets lost nor is misguided by illusion.

HARRIET: I think our individuality goes beyond that, Bob. It is our awareness that we can make decisions, including

> Through my faith I know I am unique, that God loves me.
> (Martin)

decisions whether to believe in God or not. It's an awareness that every decision we make is our own and has the potential to change something. I don't know if my talking to you will change anything you think or do, but when I decided to speak just now, I know there is the potential to change something outside of myself. Everything I do has that potential. Even if I order tea instead of coffee or a soda, I am making a decision about what I think is best for me, and that decision has a tiny impact not only on this café's business but even on world commerce. I know this impact is miniscule, but it's there nonetheless. Also it's a decision about what I think is good for me, which may be wrong, but over time I can be aware of my health and know whether it's getting better or worse, and if it's getting worse, I can examine my eating and exercise habits and other things I do to see if I should change something. That's just a tiny piece of it. When I decided to have a child and did it, I added another human being to the planet who will do things that will change something, and his absence from the world, had I decided against having him, would mean that the world would not be the same. Of course he could have ended up being an ax murderer and then I might have regretted my decision, but I also did all I could to help him become a decent human being who would make a positive contribution to the world. So I don't think you have to believe in God or be a scientist to be aware of your individuality and affirm it, even if others might disagree with

> I think our individuality . . . is an awareness that every decision we make is our own and has the potential to change something. (Harriet)

what you do or who you are. But I agree with both of you that it's easy for the individual to get lost and become nothing more than a leaf blowing in the wind.

MARTIN: Well, I think it helps to believe in God. My relationship to God preserves my individuality.

BOB: I don't think we'll ever agree, but that's because we are three independent-minded individuals.

HARRIET: So we agree that our individuality is important, even though we have different ideas about what our individuality consists of. I guess our parents did something right. They must have guided us to respect ourselves as individuals.

BOB: Maybe that's why they stick together even though they argue all the time.

Five

MARTIN: I've actually been thinking about what you said this afternoon about individuality.

BOB: I'm surprised to hear that you are thinking about it. You seem so closed up in faith that I think you never think about what we say?

MARTIN: Do you think about what I say? You reject faith without thinking about it.

BOB: To me faith is not about thinking.

MARTIN: Well, actually it is. I had to think about it before I took the leap into faith.

BOB: But now that you have leapt into faith, why does thinking matter anymore? You said that faith is superior to rationality.

MARTIN: It is, but I have to think to explain it to others and to live in the world in accordance with God.

BOB: But why do we matter? Isn't your relationship to God enough?

MARTIN: Yes, but people still matter. I'd like others to have faith too, for their sake.

BOB: And I'd like others not to have faith, for their sake.

MARTIN: So, I was actually thinking about what you two said about individuality. I think what is missing from your views of individuality is morality, right and wrong, good and evil. Harriet, how do you know your decisions are right? Bob, what's the difference between a scientist who wants to experiment with exploding nuclear weapons on people and a scientist who is searching for a cure for cancer? It seems to me that you need God to guide you. Otherwise, anything goes.

BOB: The goal of science has always been to attain knowledge to help humanity. I agree that some scientists lose sight of that higher goal and do research because they get paid to do it and don't care about how it's going to be used. Scientists are humans too, and they need jobs. Often they let their needs and the needs of their families get in the way of the goal of science, and they do whatever research they can get paid for. So a drug company may pay a team of scientist to prove that their latest drug is effective, and if a member of that team finds that the drug has a bad side effect or is ineffective, he or she might get fired. That's when science gets corrupted. The results of science get skewed by those who can pay to get the results they want, and if there is no money to do the studies that might lead to a different result, then those studies don't get done unless someone does it on his own in a basement. So, yes, it's a problem. I just don't think believing in God solves the problem. The goal is to help humanity, and you can do that without believing in God.

MARTIN: But where does someone get the strength to go

The goal of science has always been to attain knowledge to help humanity. (Bob) against the company that employs him and risk losing his job? You need God to provide that strength.

BOB: Well, it's a good question. I don't really know where that strength comes from. Yet, people do it all the time, putting truth above their own self-interest. I don't know if whistleblowers, for example, all believe in God or exposed fraud because God told them to, or if they did it for some other reason. Maybe they did it to get a reward or publicity. My point is that you don't have to believe in God to want to do what's right for humanity.

MARTIN: In some cases successful whistleblowers do get a reward. But I know that's not so in all cases.

HARRIET: I think if you feel the preciousness of life, the desire to help others comes from that. For me, having a son was a wonderful experience, awesome. To see a new life being created and coming from my own body, it was totally amazing. So from that, it just followed that I wanted my son to live and have a life he would enjoy. But it's not just about me and him, because I can see that every parent, at least most parents, have experiences like this. I feel connected to them, because I know they—most of them—feel as I do. And then I realize that my parents, and others' parents—most of them—have had the same experiences. I see pictures of the utter misery of parents who have just lost a child, and know that they, no matter where they live in the world, feel as I do about such a loss. It's a feeling that connects me to every parent in the world, mothers and fathers, and to their

---

I think if you feel the preciousness of life, the desire to help others comes from that. (Harriet)

children. When I think about this I get teary and overwhelmed. I don't think there is a scientific explanation for this, because science generally does not consider feelings to be a part of the data that it considers to be relevant. But I consider these feelings to be the source of my humanity, and why I want to do things in the world that help others live more enjoyable lives, and live at all. So my first reaction to war is to be against it. My first reaction to people suffering is to find a way to support them and relieve their suffering. These feelings determine my politics and how I live day to day. The only way I can think of God is as the energy that connects us to one another through these feelings. That's not the God you are talking about, Mart, and it is beyond anything science has addressed.

MARTIN: I think we have to be suspicious of these feelings, because they do not distinguish good from evil. Not everything we feel is good is good, and it makes no sense to relieve the suffering of people who do evil things. How do either you or Bob know what is good for humanity? Bob, how do you know that the knowledge that science uncovers is good for humanity? You both are living on faith. Harriet, your faith is in your feelings, and Bob, your faith is in science. You need another faith, faith in God, to know right from wrong.

HARRIET: As I said before, there is a difference between faith and trust. Trust in a particular thing can be refuted by that thing doing something that makes it unworthy of trust. Trust is open to experience, and I'm open to seeing how my actions affect others and to whether what I do has the effects I desire. I don't have faith in anything or anyone. But I do have trust. I start with trust and remain open to experience to decide whether the trust should be continued in particular situations.

BOB: I think Harriet is right about trust. My belief in the value of science is trust, not faith. I trust that knowledge is always a good thing, but I am aware that sometimes certain kinds of knowledge do not deserve to be trusted. I don't want a stranger to know so much about me that they can steal my identity or know when I am away from home on vacation so they can break in and steal my stuff. So not all knowledge serves humanity.

MARTIN: But Bob, how you determine what is good for humanity? Why do you think that you as an individual can do that or even have the right to do it?

BOB: Every individual has to decide that for himself or herself. There is no escape from that.

HARRIET: I agree that the decision rests with each individual. It's a burden of being alive, to have the responsibility to make these decisions.

MARTIN: I think these decisions have to come from God, but the only way to know what they are is to have faith in God. Without that faith, it's every man, every person for him or herself.

BOB: Well, once again we find ourselves at an impasse. We all have different views.

HARRIET: At least we can talk about it without killing each other. It's late, time for me to go to bed.

MARTIN: We can't kill each other. We are family, brother and sister, sitting here in the living room of our sleeping parents.

BOB: I hope that's not the only reason for not killing each other.

HARRIET: Actually, we have something in common. We

seem to agree that our individuality is important, whether it's a relationship to God, connection to our feelings and the ability to make decisions, or as inquirers who can discover things others haven't. Flowing with the crowd doesn't seem to be our thing.

MARTIN: So Harriet, does that explain the ugly shoes you are wearing?

HARRIET: Absolutely. I hate fashion. These shoes are comfortable. I don't care what they look like to others. Good night.

Six

HARRIET: This coffee shop is perfect for this rainy morning.

BOB: Plus we can snack all morning. As much as I love the park, I get hungry on those walks.

MARTIN: And I can drink coffee all morning.

HARRIET: We can eat and drink and get fat.

BOB: We can go on a long hike this afternoon if it stops raining and use up all the calories we consumed this morning.

HARRIET: And when you get hungry, eat a carrot.

BOB: Blcah!

MARTIN: I'd rather eat another donut.

HARRIET: That's why your tummy is getting a little big. But I can't talk, so let's change the subject.

MARTIN: OK. You still haven't answered my question about how you distinguish right from wrong. You need God to do that.

You still haven't answered my question about how you distinguish right from wrong. You need God to do that.
(Martin)

BOB: No, you need a community of inquirers who discuss the facts and findings and attempt to reach a consensus. It needs to be a world-wide community to avoid nationalistic bias; it needs to be women and men to avoid gender bias, and it needs to include all major ethnic groups. What binds them together should be adherence to the scientific method, which confirms all ideas with experience.

MARTIN: So your community of inquirers excludes God, so it will not have any moral guidance.

BOB: You can't confirm God with experience, so God is out. That's not to say that the inquirers themselves can't believe in God. That's a separate individual matter. But ideas that can't be confirmed by experience would be tossed out as irrelevant, God included, as far as this community is concerned. Truth, right and wrong, would be the result of the consensus of this community, subject to change as we experience new and different things.

HARRIET: But Bob, that may be fine over the course of a few centuries. We all live in the present and have to make decisions at nearly every moment. We can't wait for a consensus of the world-wide community of inquirers to make personal decisions, like whether to have a child, like who to vote for, like how to respond to an attack, like how to help someone in need, even like what to eat for lunch.

BOB: Well, we have to make decisions based on what we

No, you need a community of inquirers who discuss the facts and findings and attempt to reach a consensus. . . . What binds them together should be adherence to the scientific method. (Bob) know at the time. True, the world-wide community of inquirers that I envision does not now exist, but thousands of smaller inquiring communities exist and have existed for a long time, international communities. These communities have provided you with the information you need to make informed personal decisions. They also have provided the knowledge for technological advances to help us accomplish what we want to accomplish. Say you see someone with an apparent heart attack. Inquirers over many decades have arrived at the knowledge to inform you about what to do, and the technology to do it, if it's available. If nothing else, you dial 911 and an ambulance will come while you perform CPR to keep the person alive. Decades ago there was no phone, no 911 to call even after there were phones. If someone went to get the doctor, he'd have to get on a horse or run, and if the doctor was visiting someone else, there might be no way to find him. By the time the doctor got there, the man would be dead. So these communities of inquirers over decades and centuries have given us a greater ability to accomplish what we want, to keep the man alive after he has a heart attack. That's just an example. As the result of other communities of inquirers, your life is less in danger if you have baby, and the baby is much more likely to survive. Now you can even get data on local hospitals and choose one that seems to provide the safest setting for childbirth, and you can determine the risks of a home birth if you want to consider that. As the results of other communities of inquirers, when you go eat

We can't wait for a consensus of the world-wide community of inquirers to make personal decisions.
(Harriet)

lunch you can know what foods are best for you and what to avoid.

HARRIET: That's why I said eat a carrot instead of a donut.

BOB: Well, I don't have to follow the best advice. I'd rather have a donut. It's still a personal decision.

HARRIET: But Bob, are you saying that if people have the information they need they will usually make the best decision?

BOB: Basically, yes. I believe that if everyone was properly informed by the latest information from all communities of inquirers, that most people would make the best decisions most of the time. I know it's not perfect, because knowledge grows and changes. Many years ago the latest nutritional information available to us indicated that it wasn't good to eat eggs at all. Then a few years later the same inquiring communities said it was OK for most people to eat eggs occasionally, and now, as far as I know, it's OK for almost anybody to eat eggs if they are not allergic to them, and eggs are good for you in moderate quantities. So these communities do not get it right all the time, but since religion is not involved, they change their minds based on new studies and new information. Over time, they will get closer and closer to the truth. Meanwhile, the wise thing to do is to know about the latest information so that we can make the best decisions. And that's possible because other communities of inquirers have given us the information needed to create new things.

> I believe that if everyone was properly informed by the latest information from all communities of inquirers, that most people would make the best decisions most of the time. (Bob)

Centuries ago it was the printing press, today the Internet, tomorrow who knows what, but it is these communities of inquirers that now make it possible for anyone to get the information needed to make informed and reasonable decisions and to develop the technology to accomplish what we want to accomplish.

MARTIN: So why do people still smoke when they know it's bad for them?

BOB: First of all, fewer people smoke, and secondly, too many people still are not properly informed, and thirdly, once you are hooked, it's hard to quit. That's why cigarette companies are targeting young kids to get them hooked before they know any better and selling tobacco in countries with poor education. But increasingly smoking is being banned in public places. That was unthinkable a while ago. Based on what we have known for decades, smoking should have been banned in public places by 1950 if not sooner. Commercial interests got in the way of public health. But it's finally happening, and we have the communities of inquirers who discovered the bad health effects of tobacco to thank for this.

HARRIET: But Bob, aren't you relying on faith to say that most people will make the right decisions most of the time if they are properly informed?

BOB: No, it's not faith. I consider it a working hypothesis which can be tested with experience over time. I do believe it to be true, but I am also open to having this belief tested. Even if I eat a donut instead of a carrot, I think most of the time I make better decisions, because I am informed about the consequences of my decisions and the alternatives. I don't think it's faith or even trust, but just that we have to have working hypotheses to live. As long as we are open to having these hypotheses tested, I think that's the way to live.

MARTIN: So I've heard about experiments where decent people are given the ability to administer shocks to another, fully knowing that it hurts those getting the shocks, and they increase the shocks and seem to enjoy doing so. I think that disproves your hypothesis.

BOB: I don't think it disproves it, but maybe it is evidence against it. I'd like to know more about the people chosen for those experiments and about what they know. I'd also like to know more about the researchers. There are always people trying to prove that we are basically evil, since that's what religion tries to teach us, just like there are scientists hired by cigarette companies to prove that smoking isn't going to hurt you. Besides, there's evidence going the other way. There are people who risk their own lives to save another, even when the person being saved is a stranger to them. People will risk getting burned to pull someone out of a burning car, or risk getting drowned to pull someone out of a river. Some researchers will spend their entire lives looking for a cure for cancer. Why do they do this? So I think there is more evidence supporting my hypothesis than against it.

MARTIN: I suspect most of the people doing the right thing were guided by their faith in God.

BOB: I suspect some of those people administering shocks believed in God too.

HARRIET: Hey, you are both speculating. I'm not sure you can prove anything about believing in God. Just because someone says they believe in God does not mean that they do. They may not even be lying, because they may believe they believe but don't know what it really means to believe. Or they may believe in God like I do or some other way and not like the way Martin does. So I doubt you can really test people's behavior based on their beliefs in God, because how do you really know what they believe?

BOB: It would be especially hard if God doesn't exist.

MARTIN: Your whole assumption is that you cannot experience God. But that assumption is false. If you have faith in God, you experience God. You can't experience God without faith.

BOB: But that's circular.

MARTIN: Yes, but you are circular too. You can't experience God because you don't have faith and don't want to.

BOB: But why should I want to experience God when I don't believe God exists? I have no desire to believe in an illusion.

MARTIN: I think it's better to believe in God and have God's guidance about good and evil instead of living under your working hypothesis that might be wrong.

BOB: I'd rather live under my working hypothesis that might be wrong but can be tested than to be guided by an illusion.

HARRIET: We always end up with an impasse. It's a good time to take a break from this conversation, because I need a snack and a carrot won't do by itself. But I do find it interesting. Your views about faith and science and communities of inquirers really make me think about the roles of others in our lives and how what they have done over

> Your whole assumption is that you cannot experience God.... If you have faith in God, you experience God.
> (Martin)

centuries influences us. It makes me think about civilization itself, especially one that contains both religion and science, and how we take for granted the creations of others that totally change our lives. I wonder what we have done or will do that will change the lives of others. And who prepared the meal we are going to eat, and where did the food come from, each ingredient, the salt, the sugar, the grains, the vegys, the many spices, the gasoline to transport it and the metals and plastics in the vehicles that transported it and the creation and design of the vehicles themselves and all of their many parts? There are others who work and worked in the past to bring us to today. And that's just a tiny bit of what we take for granted. Kids today don't even know what a typewriter is, but that's where the keyboard design came from. This is fascinating when you think about it. It's like we are in a vast sea created by others, but we are also part of creating the sea.

I'd rather live under my working hypothesis that might be wrong but can be tested than to be guided by an illusion.
(Bob)

Seven

MARTIN: Ahh, I love walking in the park after the rain. It's steamy but the air is fresh, it's breezy, it's a little cooler. It feels good to breathe.

HARRIET: Yes, the rain washed away all of that air pollution.

BOB: And the pollen. I can breathe without sneezing.

MARTIN: You should take an antihistamine.

BOB: I'd rather sneeze. Every antihistamine I take makes me feel either drowsy or tired or fogs my mind.

MARTIN: That's odd. They don't bother me at all.

HARRIET: Just shows how we are all different. Most people can take aspirin but if I take even half an aspirin my nose bleeds.

MARTIN: You're weird.

HARRIET: I know, but that's who I am. I have to respect that.

MARTIN: So Bob, what does your community of inquirers have to say about Harriet who's weird?

BOB: I remember many years ago people were advised to take daily a low dosage of aspirin to prevent heart attacks.

Then they discovered that a small percentage of the population has the kind of problem Harriet has. So we discovered that some people are weird, like Harriet.

HARRIET: I remember that, and I started taking aspirin as soon as I heard it might prevent heart attacks. But I quit after a couple of weeks after reducing my dosage and still getting nose bleeds. I didn't learn until much later that your community of inquirers had discovered that a small percentage of the population are like me and shouldn't take aspirin regularly, even in low dosages. But I didn't wait for them to find this out. I made my own decisions based on my own experience. At the time I thought I was the only person in the world who got nosebleeds from taking aspirin. And I quit without relying on someone else telling me that, yes, some others are like me too. So that's just one example of why I think your theory, Bob, about a community of inquirers—while it sounds good, and I really don't disagree with it—leaves something out. Sometimes an individual has to decide for him or herself what to do without confirmation from anyone else.

MARTIN: I agree. When you have faith in God, you can get God's guidance and be guided by God, not by others.

HARRIET: Well, I didn't ask for God's guidance. I relied on my own experience. It didn't matter to me what God would say or what the community of inquirers would say. I decided on my own that it was best for me not to take aspirin on a regular basis. I haven't taken one since I quit. Only later did

---

Sometimes an individual has to decide for him or herself what to do without confirmation from anyone else.
(Harriet)

the community of inquirers say, "Oh yeah, you are probably one of those outliers we found out about." I couldn't wait for that.

MARTIN: What gives you the right to make these decisions?

HARRIET: Well, I've been making them all my life and no one has arrested me and no lightning has stuck me down. Aspirin is just an example. Basically I make my own decisions based on my own experience that takes into consideration the knowledge that is out there to the extent I am aware of it. It's not about having the right; it's about who I am as an individual. It's about being true to myself and relying on what I experience.

BOB: But do you allow that what you may experience— that is, what you think you are experiencing— may be wrong? That's why you need others to share your experiences with and get some assurance that you are not a crazy loon. Like maybe the nosebleeds were caused by something else you were doing.

HARRIET: It depends on what it is. With the aspirin, I tried it for a few days and got nosebleeds. Then I stopped and the nosebleeds stopped. Then I tried it again for a few days, and got nosebleeds. I stopped and the nosebleeds stopped. I did this a third time, reducing the dosage each time, and got the same results. So this did not absolutely prove that the aspirin and not something else was causing my nosebleeds, but it was enough evidence for me to act on. At that point, what

When you have faith in God, you can get God's guidance and be guided by God, not by others. (Martin)

others might have experienced became irrelevant. I have to accept that my body is not someone else's body, and that what I experience with my body may not be experienced by anyone else. But I accept that I have to be careful about what causes what, because it's easy to think one thing causes another when it's actually something else. But when it comes to my own body or even my own way of thinking and believing, I believe that I am unique and what others experience might not be relevant to me, though it is relevant to them. It's different if I am talking about something outside of me. I'd be wrong to say that since aspirin causes me to have nosebleeds that it causes someone else to have nosebleeds. When it comes to what affects others, I agree with you, Bob, that I have to listen to what others have experienced, including the findings of some of your communities of inquirers. So what I'm saying is that there is a difference between what I decide about what's right for me and what I think about is right for others, because the two are not the same.

MARTIN: I still think that neither of you can know what is right or wrong without God's guidance. Harriet, what keeps you from deciding that what is best for you is to kill someone else?

HARRIET: I start with my awareness of my own decision-making power. I have the power at every moment to make a decision that will affect the rest of my life and will affect others. Right at this moment I am deciding to be here instead of some place else. Every moment I decide whether to

You need others to share your experiences with and get some assurance that you are not a crazy loon. (Bob)

continue living or find some way to end it all. Every decision I make at every moment determines my future and affects the future of others. This is an awesome power. In a way it is the power we attribute to God, the power to change the present that changes the future. But this power is within me, and within each of us. This is why I think of God as not existing outside of ourselves but as being within us, within each of us—it is this awesome power to continually make decisions, and each decision in some way affects the universe. The more I am aware of this power within me, I have to assume that others have the same power. If I kill someone else, I would be destroying a unique source of this power within that person. To me this power within every person is beautiful. Instead of wanting to destroy it, I want to interact with it and help others use their power in ways that help others use their power, and so on. It is a beautiful thing when people do this for each other. When that happens, we are loving our own power and loving that power in others. We nurture each other by loving this power within each of us. I don't know if this is God or not, but I think of it as Godly energy because it is awesome and beautiful. It is the energy, the loving power within each of us. So, Mart, what is right is to nurture this power within each of us, and what is wrong is to destroy it or stifle it.

MARTIN: But some people use this power to kill others. What is so beautiful about that?

HARRIET: Yes, and it's awful. I think people who kill others were brought up, perhaps brutally, so that they became blind to the beauty and awesomeness of this power in themselves as well as in others. They are alienated from their own decision making power and so aren't aware of it in others. They substitute for their own decision making power, power over others, and others to them are just things who compete with them for the earth's goodies. Killing means nothing to them, because others are things that exist for them either only for their own pleasure or as impediments to their pleasure. So, my way of looking at it is that killing another is to kill the Godly energy within the victim. Those who kill are alienated from this energy and disconnected from this energy within others.

MARTIN: So you would kill those who kill others to protect what you call Godly energy?

HARRIET: No, not if there is another way. Those who kill still have this Godly energy within them, so I do not want to destroy that energy by killing them. Still, at times it might be necessary to kill someone to prevent that person from killing others. I want to protect myself from being killed, and I will do whatever I have to do to protect myself, even if I have to kill the attacker. But I think in most cases there is another way. If I can escape or disable the attacker enough to get away, that's what I'll do. But if my efforts to protect myself result in the death of the attacker and there was no other way, then I think I'm justified to do what I can to protect myself.

BOB: At least the law recognizes the right of self-defense.

HARRIET: Well it's kind of an ethical or moral right too.

> I think of God as not existing outside of ourselves but as being within us, within each of us—it is this awesome power to continually make decisions.... If I kill someone else, I would be destroying a unique source of this power within that person. (Harriet)

There is no reason not to want to preserve what is most precious to us, our own lives. We are also faced with the dilemma of what to do to save the lives of others. Do we jeopardize our own lives to do so? I think I wouldn't hesitate to jeopardize my own life to save my son. But to go to war to save whatever, I'm not so sure about that. Every time it's come up during my life, I say no way. Most of these wars are to get or protect territory or natural resources or gain economic advantage, and the people are beside the point. But I can't say it would never be justified.

MARTIN: So that's why you are against the death penalty? This is where we disagree about right and wrong. People who kill for no reason are evil and should be removed from the earth. If they aren't removed, they will kill others. Some people, like Hitler, deserve to die and should be killed. You wouldn't kill Hitler; you'd let him live.

HARRIET: I'm not so sure I would not have killed Hitler, if I had had the chance.

BOB: Actually, I think killing Hitler would have been beside the point. Hitler would not have had any power if people did not follow him. Hitler was not the problem. The problem was the people who followed him and those who kept silent if they didn't follow him. When we think of Hitler as an evil person who should have been killed, we forget that the only thing that made him evil was that people supported him or acquiesced. So are we going to say that all of his supporters and inactive opponents were evil. Then we'd have

---

People who kill for no reason are evil.... Some people, like Hitler, deserve to die and should be killed. (Martin)

to kill all of them if we think Hitler should be killed. If we killed them all, that would be the crime of genocide. Then we, the killers, would be the evil, as far as I'm concerned. So Mart, what does your God say about that?

HARRIET: Well, give Mart some time to think about that. It's interesting that you and I agree about this, but I'm not too surprised, since I always thought of you as a peaceful person. What has always troubled me was that those fighting against Hitler indiscriminately bombed Dresden. They also fire bombed Tokyo and then dropped two atomic bombs on Japan, which were attacks on the civilian populace that killed hundreds of thousands of people in the blink of an eye. It's not that the civilians were incidentally killed while attacking the military. The civilians were intentionally targeted. I wonder if in the minds of those who ordered those attacks, whether they were thinking that the populace was to blame for supporting their rulers, so that they should be killed too. These bombings were, to me, genocidal attacks, and had the war not ended, these bombings of civilians would have continued, I'm sure. So where is the evil here? It seems like it's spread out to all sides.

BOB: The American public supported those bombings, and if anyone opposed them, they were silent, just like the Germans. So if Hitler was evil, not only were the German people evil for supporting him, the American people, the British, and so on were also evil to support their bombings which intentionally decimated vast civilian populations. It

Hitler would not have had any power if people did not follow him. (Bob)

doesn't make sense to say all these evil people should be killed. It makes more sense to question whether anyone should be killed and whether anyone is really evil, or more evil than the rest us.

MARTIN: I think when you lose your faith in God that you end up in these quandaries. Hitler was the leader, so that's where the source of the evil is. He and Japan started wars. We responded and did what was necessary to end it. You can't get rid of evil by wishing it wasn't there. It's there and always has been there. When you have faith in God, you are guided to do what is right and oppose evil.

HARRIET: But Mart, there is a difference between saying there is evil and saying that certain people are evil and should be killed. People do things that hurt others, sometimes intentionally and sometimes inadvertently. Just because they do bad things does not make them evil.

MARTIN: So you would get rid of all the laws that define what is right and what isn't? You wouldn't put people in jail who commit crimes? To you, maybe there are no crimes, because everyone is basically good.

BOB: I think she is saying that people are not basically anything, good or evil. It's what they do that matters, not whether they are good or evil. Am I putting words in your mouth, Harriet?

HARRIET: Well, yes and no. I don't know what people basically are, but I do know I tend to trust that they will do the right thing until experience shows otherwise. Whenever I drive and face oncoming traffic, I trust that no one will swerve in front of me. If I didn't have that trust, I couldn't drive. I'd be too scared. Still I know that now and then someone does swerve into oncoming traffic and kills someone or gets killed. So I always look at the oncoming traffic to see if I see erratic behavior that would put me on notice that someone is drunk or asleep or having a heart attack. I also watch the rear view mirror when I come to a stop and try to give myself enough room to get out of the way if I think the driver behind me is texting and not paying attention. When I stop at a stop light and the light turns green, I trust that the people facing a red light will stop, but I also look first to see if someone is not paying attention and not stopping. None of this has to do with whether people are good or evil. If someone runs a red light and crashes into someone and kills them, it doesn't mean he was evil. He did a bad thing and maybe committed a crime and goes to jail. I'm not against jails or prisons. We need them to keep some people who can't be trusted off the streets so they don't hurt someone else. So I'm not against laws that are designed to protect us. But none of this requires that we think of people as basically good or evil. It's all about what they do and what should be done to protect ourselves and others. Once someone is in prison and can't hurt anybody else, there's no point in killing him. You don't kill someone who can't hurt you.

MARTIN: So what about Hitler? You are saying he wasn't evil.

BOB: Look, if killing Hitler would have stopped the war, fine, do it. But since Hitler had millions of followers, it wouldn't have done any good to kill Hitler. You just would

---

There is a difference between saying there is evil and saying that certain people are evil and should be killed.
(Harriet)

have made him a martyr and strengthened the resolve of his followers to get revenge. Instead of ending the war, it might have lengthened the war. People are mistaken to think that killing the evil leader solves anything. Leaders don't exist without followers. If the leader is killed, the followers will erect another leader to follow and keep doing what they have been doing.

MARTIN: So logically you should kill the followers.

BOB: Logically, yes, that's the problem. But to kill the followers who may be just civilians is to commit the same evil we are trying to get rid of.

MARTIN: I think if you keep killing the leaders, the followers would soon give up.

BOB: If some enemy killed the President, and then killed the next President then the next President, do you think the American people would give up? I don't think so. I don't think we are that different from others. Hitler still has followers today, people who admire him and others who are like him. They haven't given up. I have no idea why anyone would be so sick as to admire Hitler, but they exist. I don't understand it.

MARTIN: Maybe your community of inquirers will figure it out some day.

BOB: Maybe they will.

HARRIET: And until then, we have to figure out what to do. Still, there is something about Bob's community of inquirers that is appealing. It is open ended, committed to

---

People are mistaken to think that killing the evil leader solves anything. Leaders don't exist without followers.
(Bob)

understanding based on sound methodology, and this methodology is the means for peacefully settling disputes. I think this idea of a community of inquirers could be a model for other kinds of communities. So I'm not at all against the idea of communities analogous to Bob's vision. Actually I like the idea. But many communities are united by hate of outsiders. We could do without them. Ultimately the individual has to make decisions, with or without the support of a community, and these decisions have to be made all the time, many times a day. And the individual has to decide what kind of communities to be a part of.

BOB: I think the community of inquirers is quite consistent with individual decision making, but you do have a point that sometimes we have to act without any community support. But to the extent what we do impacts others, it's good to have community input about what we do, and the community of inquirers is, to me, the best approach to making these kinds of decision. Speaking of individual decision-making, what I want to do now is go home and take a nap. Maybe I'll dream the answer of how the community and individual should relate.

MARTIN: If you do, it may be God speaking to you. Be sure to remember the dream.

BOB: So God even speaks to the faithless?

MARTIN: Sometimes. Be sure to listen.

Eight

HARRIET: So, Bob, did God speak to you in your dreams during your nap?

BOB: Well, if He did, I can't remember, and the solution to the world's problems has been lost forever.

MARTIN: Even if God did speak to you, you would assume you were hallucinating and dismiss it.

BOB: Yep, you're right.

HARRIET: So Mart, why doesn't God tell you the solution? Surely He knows. And if He is good, He will tell us the answer, and tell it to someone like you who believes.

MARTIN: God decided to give us free will. It's that decision-making power you were talking about, Harriet. That power can only come from God. He chose to give it to us. He chose to let us decide whether to pursue God or to pursue evil.

BOB: So Hitler was God's responsibility? He created us so that Hitler and others like him could pursue evil? I don't get it.

MARTIN: We are mere humans and cannot understand the ways of God. Since God gave us free will, we are free to have faith in God or to pursue evil. So Hitler and those like him chose evil. He left it to us who have faith to decide what to do about it.

HARRIET: But didn't Hitler believe in God?

MARTIN: Those who pursue evil often claim to be doing what God wants. What do you expect an evil person to do? You couldn't expect Hitler to stand before the crowds and tell the people, "Folks, I've decided to reject God and pursue evil." I think the crowds would have dispersed at that point. No, those who are evil have to claim that they believe in God and are doing God's will.

BOB: So if the leader says he or she is following the will of God, how are we to know?

MARTIN: You can't know based on what they say. You have to ask for God's guidance.

HARRIET: So you are saying that we have to question our leaders?

MARTIN: No, I am saying that you have to ask for God's guidance whether to trust your leader. If God guides you to trust your leader, then you follow the leader.

BOB: But didn't Hitler's followers do just that?

MARTIN: I have no idea. But I suspect they just followed the leader without asking God whether the leader should be followed. I think that's why people follow evil leaders. They don't ask for God's guidance but accept their leader as though he were God.

BOB: But we don't know that for sure. Too bad we couldn't have interviewed all those people. But even if we

---

God decided to give us free will.... He chose to let us decide whether to pursue God or to pursue evil. (Martin)

could have done so, it would be hard to account for faulty memories, lying, and honest but creative interpretations of the past. We'd have to interview them at the time they were supporting Hitler and hook them to lie detectors at the same time. Lie detectors didn't even exist then, I don't think. But we have had many similar situations since then. I just don't see how we could find out whether the people who were following their leader checked with God to see if they should trust the leader. I'm sure they wouldn't agree to be hooked up to lie detectors.

HARRIET: Pollsters assume most of those surveyed will tell the truth.

BOB: On some issues, I think that's a faulty assumption. Most people don't like being outliers, unlike you, Harriet. They want to go along with the majority, especially if it's an overwhelming majority. If you asked most people today whether they believed in God, a lot of them would say "Yes" even if they have doubts. They don't want to be outliers. So I guess what I'm getting at, Mart, is that there is no way really to know whether people who follow their leader do so only after asking God if they should. So solid evidence to support the idea that God will correctly tell us whether to follow our leader probably cannot be gotten.

MARTIN: There you go, confusing science with faith. You are looking for scientific proof whether it makes sense to believe in God. You can't get that proof. You either have faith or you don't. Once you have faith, the kind of proof you are looking for is irrelevant. It's relevant to you, because you don't have faith.

BOB: Are you saying that if you have faith, you don't need to prove God's existence?

MARTIN: Actually, yes, that's right. Those who are trying to prove the existence of God don't have faith. If you have faith, proof is irrelevant. With faith, you know God exists. Without faith, you don't. When you don't have faith, you look to proofs.

BOB: Seems to me that faith creates God in the mind of the one with faith. Faith doesn't connect you to God; it only connects you to your belief in God. Whether there is a being that corresponds to that belief can never be known.

MARTIN: That's the way it will seem to someone who does not have faith.

HARRIET: So you are both caught up in your own circles. If you have faith, God exists no matter what. If you don't have faith, nothing can prove that God exists.

BOB: Right. Since I see no reason to have faith, God will never exist for me.

MARTIN: That's a shame.

BOB: I'm quite happy without faith. It's not a shame at all. Actually, I think people are better off without faith. If you don't have faith, you don't get misled by tyrants who say they are following the will of God. And you don't assume that those who disagree with you or don't like you are evil people who oppose God, since there is no God. I think if we all agreed long ago that God does not exist, Hitler could not have gotten the following he got, and all these tyrants who say they are abiding by God's commands would be ignored or seen as fools. You see, to go to war to destroy the evil enemy you have

---

Those who are trying to prove the existence of God don't have faith.... When you don't have faith, you look to proofs. (Martin)

to believe that there is a God that the evil opposes. If there is no God, there is no evil to destroy. Instead, we are all just people with different points of view. We'd have to figure out a way to get along with one another. So I think that without God, we'd all be better off.

MARTIN: So wouldn't people still kill each other to get what they want? You have a supply of meat and I'm hungry, so I kill you to get the meat. Or my lover gets attracted to someone else, so I kill them both. It happens all the time. Getting rid of God won't stop people from killing each other. Instead, you need fear of God to keep people in line. If you know that God disapproves of killing, then that's what will stop you from killing.

BOB: What will stop people from killing one another is getting together to reach agreements and establish laws that we should follow, and those who don't follow the law are punished or excluded from the society. That's what all stable societies do. I don't think believing in God has anything to do with creating societies guided by laws that provide stability and order.

MARTIN: People have to believe that the laws have a higher source, that they come from God, like commandments. Otherwise they will ignore them.

BOB: I don't think so. They will abide by the laws out of self-interest, because if they don't, they will get excluded. Prisons are a way to exclude them. That's all you need. You don't need God's authority. All you need is for people to act

---

Faith doesn't connect you to God; it only connects you to your belief in God. (Bob)

out of their self-interest and establish a society with laws that protect one another.

MARTIN: So you have set up a world where the nonbelievers are good and the believers are evil.

BOB: No, the believers are not evil. They just have to abide by the laws like everyone else. Just because I disagree with them does not mean that I would exclude them. That's my point. Set up the laws needed to keep order and peace so believers and non-believers can live together without killing one another.

HARRIET: It seems to me that this is essentially what we have now, a society in which believers and non-believers live together without killing one another.

BOB: Not quite. Presidents still call upon God to go to war. When we go to war, whoever is President will at least hint that God supports us, that God believes in democracy and freedom, and ends every speech approving of war with "God bless America," implying that God does not bless the designated enemy. If we could get God out of the picture, we could look at this more objectively. Believing that there is a God who is on our side and opposes the enemy supports wars that should not be fought.

HARRIET: In my view, God does not take sides. God exists within each one of us, even those we call our enemy.

MARTIN: Sometimes God is on our side and wars have to be fought. Harriet, I still think you are saying that we should not have fought against Hitler?

HARRIET: No, I'm not saying that. But I think if we looked at Hitler and his followers, and the Japanese Emperor and his followers, as precious human beings like everyone else, we would have focused solely on what was necessary to defend ourselves and defend others against aggression and fought the war differently. For example, we would not have targeted civilians in Dresden, Tokyo, Hiroshima and Nagasaki. That was overkill, motivated by total disrespect and hatred for the people we were fighting.

MARTIN: But Hitler killed civilians. Look at all of the Jews who were killed.

HARRIET: So are you saying that we have to fight war on the terms of those we are fighting? They kill civilians, so it's OK for us to do it? That means that if the enemy is evil and we fight on their terms, we are evil too.

MARTIN: You can't be pure in war. You have to do what is necessary to win.

HARRIET: I agree that you have to do what is necessary to defend yourself and defend others from aggression, but intentional killing of civilians is not necessary. It's overkill. And when we do that, or become indifferent to the killing of civilians, or even kill soldiers when we don't have to, then we are the evil we are fighting against.

BOB: If you get God out of the picture, what Harriet is saying is right.

HARRIET: Well, God is in my picture, just not the God most people seem to believe in.

MARTIN: If God is not in the picture, then you have no moral guidance at all. You become just a floundering individual going along with the crowds.

HARRIET: I don't think you'll find either me or Bob going

In my view, God does not take sides. God exists within each one of us, even those we call our enemy. (Harriet) along with the crowds.

BOB: It's the appeal to God that creates the crowds in the first place. Without these appeals to God, people would feel freer to disagree and open to discussing opposing views. No one wants to be seen as opposing God.

MARTIN: But if God guides you to oppose the leader who is appealing to God, then you will follow God's guidance and not go along with the leader or the crowd following the leader. Crowds are created when people lose their connection to God and instead look to the leader as if he were God. God gives you the strength to oppose the crowds. If you don't believe in God, where do you get the strength to oppose the crowds and the leader?

HARRIET: My strength comes from the God within me, and I am guided to respect the God within others.

BOB: The problem only arises because people believe in God.

HARRIET: But since so many people believe in God as Martin does, what do we do?

MARTIN: I hope that question does not keep you awake all night. It's not a problem for me, so I will sleep well.

BOB: You mean it would not be a problem for you if God guided you to oppose a war that everyone else supported? You'd have a big problem.

MARTIN: Yes, but my conscience would be clear.

HARRIET: OK, I'll support your conscience.

BOB: So will I. I hope you will support ours.

Sometimes God is on our side and wars have to be fought.
(Martin)

like to leave the earth feeling that my presence here made life a little easier for someone else.

HARRIET: Can you imagine what Hitler must have felt like when he committed suicide? Everything he tried to accomplish was in ruin. I wonder if he realized that everything he stood for was wrong.

BOB: Chances are he deluded himself into believing that he'd be honored as a martyr. That's probably what most tyrants think as they die. They are so convinced that they are right, that they probably believe history will come out on their side in the end.

HARRIET: I'm sure a lot of people who do a lot of harm believe that they are doing good. They will die convinced that they were right.

BOB: But maybe that's true for all of us. How are we any different from them?

HARRIET: Well, for one thing, I am never completely convinced that I am right. I know that everything I do might have unintended consequences. So I try to observe what happens around me to see what the consequences of my actions are. If I see something that makes me think that something I did had a bad consequence, then I try to learn from that so I'd do it differently the next time so as to avoid bad consequences.

MARTIN: But how do you know what is a bad consequence and what is a good consequence? What you

---

I am never completely convinced that I am right. I know that everything I do might have unintended consequences.
(Harriet)

think is a bad consequence might actually be good. For example, what if you ran a red light and crashed into another car and injured the driver? You'd say that was a bad consequence. But what if the person you injured was on his way to kill his former girlfriend? Maybe you'd never find this out, and you'd continue to think you did a bad thing when it was actually a good thing, because it saved the life of the former girlfriend.

BOB: But maybe the former girlfriend planned to kill her children, so it would have been better if he got to her first.

MARTIN: Well, right, that is my point. How do you know what is a good consequence and what isn't?

HARRIET: So are you going to say that faith in God solves these problems?

MARTIN: Well, yes. You ask for God's guidance and trust that guidance, for otherwise you cannot know.

BOB: But so many people believe they are following God's guidance when it's clearly wrong. I still say that you cannot know when God is guiding you and when you are guided by your delusion. You can ask God whether you are doing what He wants and not being deluded, but that too could be a delusion. There is no way to know if God is guiding you or a delusion. Separating delusions from reality requires you to be constantly aware of the world around you, including the views of others. If subsequent experience or the experience of others doesn't confirm that what you are believing is true,

How do you know what is a bad consequence and what is a good consequence?... You ask for God's guidance and trust that guidance, for otherwise you cannot know. (Martin)

then you have reason to question what you believe. Questioning your own beliefs doesn't mean you say they are wrong, it just means you put question marks around them so you don't act on them until you get some kind of confirmation. So I have a problem with looking to God for confirmation, which is confirming a delusion with another delusion. Instead you have to look at the world you live in. Looking to God for the answer would just take your attention away from relating to the world. It's only your relationship to the world including other people that enables you to separate delusion from reality.

MARTIN: So Bob, don't most people believe in God? Does your relationship with them count?

BOB: I doubt that most people can agree on what God is. If someone asked you and Harriet, "Do you believe in God?" you both would say "Yes," but you have completely different ideas of what God is, so actually you do not believe in the same thing. The same is true throughout the world. You have all these different religions and different sects within each religion, so you can't say they all believe in the same God. If that were the case, they wouldn't be fighting and killing one another. So people who say, "There is no God but God," or "God is One," and stuff like that, are just blind to the reality that there really are many different views of God. On top of that, you have agnostics and atheists scattered all over the world, many of whom can't express their views without getting killed, so there must be more of them than we can

---

You cannot know when God is guiding you and when you are guided by your delusion. (Bob)

ever know. So, to answer your question, I'd say No, most people do not believe in the same God. While that does not prove that you shouldn't believe in God, all this disagreement does not support believing in God either.

MARTIN: I'm not saying that anyone should believe in God for the reason that most others do. I was only saying that your view about being aware of the world around you would lead you to believe in God because most others do, even if their views of God are not the same. I think there is only one God, and that there is no God but God, but not everyone comprehends God in the same way, and that's why there are different views of God. We are, after all, only humans with limited abilities to understand God, so it makes sense that with our limited abilities that we would have different views of something more vast than any one of us can comprehend. It's like asking all the fish in the ocean, "What is the ocean?" One fish would talk about the rocks on the bottom of the ocean that keeps it safe from bigger fish; another would know nothing about the bottom of the ocean and talk about the insects on the surface that it feeds on; and so on. Each one of us is just a fish in the ocean, and God is the ocean. None of us sees the whole ocean, so we have different views of it. But that does not mean that the ocean does not exist.

BOB: But the ocean doesn't tell the fish what is good and what is evil.

MARTIN: Well, OK, my analogy was not perfect. But you get the point.

BOB: It's an interesting analogy, but your point all along has been that you need God to tell us what is right and wrong. Using your analogy, the fish hiding under the rock would tell the fish on the surface that the right thing to do is to hide under the rock, and the fish on the surface would then have nothing to eat. And the fish on the surface would tell the fish under the rock to come to the surface for a good meal, and the fish under the rock would head for the surface and get eaten by a bigger fish. Either that, or they'd get into a big fight and kill each other, just like humans.

HARRIET: This discussion is making me hungry. Not for insects but for fish and chips.

MARTIN: OK, I guess there is no analogy to God. But I still think you get my point that God is so vast that no one can be expected to know all of God.

HARRIET: Sorry to break up the discussion. I really think knowing what is right and wrong is a fascinating question, and I'm not sure we have the answer.

BOB: It's been debated for a few millennia. We still haven't figured it out.

MARTIN: OK, so let's take a lunch break. Let's agree that when hungry, it is right to eat.

HARRIET: Yes, but what?

BOB: Carrots or donuts?

HARRIET: Fish.

MARTIN: Hamburger.

BOB: Pizza.

Ten

HARRIET: Let's go back to the coffee shop. It's still drizzling. Besides, it's a good place to continue our discussion of good and bad. It seems to me that where we left off is with the argument that believing in God does not necessarily help, because a lot of people who believe in God do the wrong thing. Waiting for Bob's world community of inquirers to decide takes too long. We all agree that just following the crowd is the wrong thing. The crowd consists mostly of people following each other just because there are a lot of them, and only a few question where the crowd is going. It seems to me that no matter how you look at it, you have to rely on your own individual judgment. Mart, you rely on your individual judgment to believe in God. Bob, you rely on your individual judgment to decide which community of inquirers is most likely to have the right answer, and you and I both rely on our individual judgment to do what we think is most likely to benefit others. I think we have to agree that our individual judgment can never know the absolute truth. We all flounder, search, make mistakes, correct them and try again. It seems to me that the biggest mistake anyone can make is to believe that they know the absolute truth and act upon that belief. Those who do that close their minds to the possibility that they may be wrong. They are the ones most likely to kill. It seems to me, as I said before, that killing another is the worst thing we can do. When you kill, you are permanently eliminating another human being from the earth. If it was a mistake, you can't correct it by bringing that person back. It's done, and no apology or retribution can retrieve the life that was taken. So I seem to be telling myself that the worst wrong is killing another, and that that is very likely to happen when the killer is convinced that he is absolutely right to kill. The next worst wrong, then, is believing that you know the absolute truth, for it is that belief that is most likely to lead you to kill.

MARTIN: I need a cup of coffee before I respond to that. Here we are; let's go in and find a comfortable place to sit.

BOB: I'll grab that table over there while you get your coffee. Meanwhile, I'll ask Harriet why she is not a pacifist, or maybe she is. I know she may have answered that before, but if so, I didn't fully understand it. I want to probe her some more.

MARTIN: No, wait until I get back. That's what I was going to ask her again, and I want to hear her answer.

HARRIET: I'm going to get some water. Bob, can I get you anything.

BOB: Thanks, but not yet. I need to let my lunch settle

A lot of people who believe in God do the wrong thing.
(Harriet)

first.

MARTIN: Ahh, I can't imagine anyone living without coffee. It tastes so good and will make me better able to think.

HARRIET: OK, so you want to know why I am not a pacifist. Some of my best friends are pacifists. No, really. I like them and respect them. I'd be quite happy in a world full of pacifists. I just have one problem. They all say that if attacked, they'd rather be killed than kill. Or they say, if someone attacked their spouse or child, they might kill as a purely emotional reaction but could not justify doing so. I have a problem with that. I view my own life as too precious to give up without a fight. If someone tried to kill me, I'd do everything I could to protect myself, and if it meant that I had to push the attacker over a cliff or stab him with a knife, I'd feel perfectly justified doing that. I'd also do everything I could to prevent an attacker from harming my child—or anyone, really. I'd try to protect myself or others without killing the attacker, but if the attacker died at my hands, I'd not have a problem with that. I'd only have a problem if I killed the attacker when there was clearly a way to escape without killing him, or if I could disable him without killing him, assuming I'm the only intended victim and no one else is going to get killed if I run away. I think my pacifists friends would have a problem in principle if I killed the attacker, even though they would probably forgive me, but I wouldn't have a problem at all if that's all I could do to save myself. Instead of feeling bad about it, I would congratulate myself for successfully fighting back. Maybe I'm a narcissist, but I think my life is too precious to give up without a fight, a big fight.

BOB: But you said it is wrong to kill. So how can you justify killing the attacker.

HARRIET: The reason it's wrong to kill is because of the preciousness of our lives, mine included. I am no less precious than the attacker, so I will defend my life from attack.

MARTIN: I think you would be right to kill the attacker. The attacker is evil and should be killed.

HARRIET: I don't believe that. Who knows what the attacker was thinking? Who am I to say that the attacker was evil? I'm not saying that it would be good that I killed the attacker. I'm just saying that my life is worth a big fight to preserve it. And that's the way I feel about everyone's life. I think it's good to preserve your own life and that of others. If the attacker gets killed when there was no other way to stop the attack, that's good, but not because it was good to kill the attacker, but because it's good to preserve my own life and that of any others being attacked.

BOB: Mart, if you say the attacker is evil, aren't you saying that you know the absolute truth, and that justifies killing the attacker?

MARTIN: I think killing is evil, and yes, to me that's an absolute.

BOB: So why isn't killing the killer evil too?

MARTIN: Those who commit evil deserve to die.

HARRIET: I don't think we have a clue about who deserves to die. I don't think anyone deserves to die. The most I can say is that our lives are precious and we need to do what is necessary to protect them. It does not follow that an attacker deserves to die. It only follows that we should do what is necessary to protect ourselves and kill attackers only if that is the only way to preserve ourselves and there was no other way. If you can disable or capture the attackers instead of killing them, or even if you can escape, that is what you should do instead. In other words, never intend to kill someone, but if you kill an attacker when there is no other way to protect yourself, then that's what you should do without accusing the attacker of being evil. Just because I deserve to live does not mean that the attacker deserved to die.

BOB: So how do you translate that personal level to the international level? Let's say a terrorist group thinks America is evil and seeks to destroy the country. Shouldn't we then support the government's attempt to destroy the terrorist group?

MARTIN: Absolutely.

BOB: I'm asking Harriet.

HARRIET: This may sound crazy, but I think you have to start by realizing that the terrorists are people who think that they are doing the right thing. At the same time, the nation has to protect itself. So I think you have to approach it simultaneously in two ways. One thing you do is to do what you need to do to prevent an attack, using infiltrators or spying devices to get information about what they are doing and who they are, and capturing them before they can act. You try to capture them without killing them, and you treat them like anyone else accused of crime, under law, because you can't know for sure that you've captured the right people. The other thing you do is to try to understand why they think as they do. They are, after all, people who have been taught certain things and who are doing what they think is right. We need to find out why they think that way. It's even possible that they have a point of view that is not absurd, and if so, we should find out what it is and try to respond in some rational way so as to dissuade others from joining them. If we just kill them, that doesn't convince others that we are right and they are wrong. It might do just the opposite.

MARTIN: If they are terrorists, they should be killed.

HARRIET: No, they are accused of crimes and should be captured and brought to trial in a fair court of justice. Ideally you want it to be an internationally recognized court of law. Simply assassinating them is wrong.

BOB: What if they try to kill you when you try to capture them?

HARRIET: If we have enough evidence to capture them, it's just like trying to capture anyone accused of crime. If they shoot at you when you try to capture them, you do what is necessary to preserve your own lives. Sometimes you have to shoot back, but often you don't need to shoot back. Instead, surround them and isolate them, block off their supplies of food and ammunition, and eventually they will surrender or commit suicide. The goal is to capture them alive and bring them to trial, just like anyone else accused of crime.

MARTIN: What if it's a whole nation that is trying to attack us?

HARRIET: Well, you don't start by dropping an atomic bomb on them! If they are actually invading, you fight back to defend yourself. If they are a threat to attack but not actually doing it, you try to get international support to isolate them, prevent them from getting the weapons and fuel they need to wage war. If you can't get that international support, then there is a bigger problem, because that means other nations either agree with the attackers or sympathize with them. However you deal with the problem, you've got to start out with the premise that the attackers are human beings like ourselves who think they are doing the right thing, that they are not evil, but that nonetheless we have to do what is necessary to protect ourselves consistent with recognizing the humanity of the attackers.

MARTIN: But if the attackers are evil, I think you need to attack them and kill them.

BOB: I think the problem is that you can't know they are evil. If you think they are evil, it's because you believe that they are acting against God's will, and that's why I don't believe in God, because without God, you have to deal with international conflict in a different way, in accordance with agreed-upon international laws.

MARTIN: But if you do believe in God, and you believe the attackers are evil, then you kill them.

HARRIET: I think the Presidents we have had would agree with you, Mart. I think Bob and I are the outliers. But since I believe in the equality of all, and that God resides within each of us, I'm a dissenter when it comes to most wars. In every war I can think of, at some point we stopped being defenders and became aggressors against civilians, killed prisoners and ignored international law.

BOB: And with no God, I end up agreeing with Harriet, even though we think about this differently.

HARRIET: So Bob, why do you agree?

BOB: In the absence of God, I think all we can do is try to reach agreements with others. Efforts to establish international law are efforts to get those agreements. That's the best we can do, and that's what we have to keep trying to do. There is no source of absolute good or evil, there is only what we can agree upon, and when we disagree, we have to discuss our disagreements and seek a common ground. It's a long, historical process and we have a long way to go to get to an international common ground, but that's what we have to do.

MARTIN: And when the terrorists attack, what do you do?

BOB: Protect ourselves, like Harriet said, but continually strive for international agreements.

MARTIN: I think you need guidance from God to distinguish good agreements from bad agreements.

BOB: I don't think we can know that, so we have to assume that the best agreements are those that include the most people, as long as the rights of the dissenters are protected. We have to assume that everyone gets the same rights, because we have no basis for thinking otherwise.

HARRIET: So you and I get to the same place, it seems. You think we have to assume all people are equal, because we don't have a good reason to prove that we are not all equal, and I say that we are all equal, because there is a bit of God within each one of us that makes everyone's life precious. This presence of God within all of us is why I'm against targeting people to kill and oppose the death penalty.

BOB: I think you can justify killing someone if that's the only way to prevent that person from killing others, but only then. You can't show that in the case of a prisoner who is confined and helpless. Another reason for not killing a convicted prisoner is that the finding of guilt may have been an error that is later reversed, but you can't reverse death.

MARTIN: I accept that our lives are precious and that God made us all equal, but you relinquish your claim to equality if

---

In the absence of God, I think all we can do is try to reach agreements with others. (Bob)

you kill another. So someone who kills another, not in self-defense, becomes unequal and deserves to be killed. Like I said before, God gave us free will, which means we can choose evil over good. Killing another is to choose evil over good. When they choose evil they become evil, and we have a right to destroy evil and kill those who are evil.

BOB: But you assume you can know who is evil and who isn't with such certainty that you know who to kill.

MARTIN: That's where I'd ask for God's guidance.

HARRIET: Oh dear, we continue to go around in circles, each of us within his own circle and no way to say which circle is the right one.

BOB: Right. That's my point, really. We are ignorant. We create circles of rational explanations to convince us that we are right, but it's just one big circle based on assumptions that can't be proven unless you are in the same circle. That's why we have to assume that there is no higher right other than what we agree upon. We can't assume we are right in some higher sense, because we just don't know and can't know.

MARTIN: That's the reason for faith. You leap out of your self-affirming meaningless circles of rationality by taking the leap of faith into the hands of God. Rationality can't give you certainty, but faith can.

BOB: But to me I'd be leaping into the hands of nothing, because there is no God there.

MARTIN: If you leap, God is there.

BOB: I have no reason to leap.

I think you need guidance from God to distinguish good
agreements from bad agreements. (Martin)

HARRIET: I'm not convinced that these circles of rationality are fully self-enclosed circles. I think there are experiences that favor one circle over another, and that the experiences are real regardless of what circle you are in.

MARTIN: Harriet, you are beginning to sound like Bob. But I think the circle determines what you experience. You can't escape these circles.

BOB: Well, if the circle determines all experience, then we are in a pickle and the scientific method is phony. I'm not ready to go there. I think the scientific method is legitimate and maybe it has an application beyond science, or what we think of as science.

HARRIET: Bob, I'd like to discuss this some more, but my mind is shot for now. Let's wait until after dinner, if you can do it then.

BOB: That's fine with me. It might help if I had a glass of wine with dinner, and maybe a cordial afterward.

MARTIN: That might be good for all of us.

HARRIET: Sounds good to me.

Eleven

HARRIET: So it seems to me that what gets you out of circles of rationality is experience. Bob, isn't that what science is about?

BOB: Absolutely. That is what experiments and factual studies are all about. Whatever conceptualization you have, whether you call it a theory, an hypothesis, or an idea, you have to confirm it with experience before it can become something to hang your hat on. Einstein's theory of relativity meant nothing until experiments were performed that supported it. Now even that theory is being questioned by new experiments. A chemist's idea of a pill that will cure a particular disease means nothing until the pill is tested and compared to a placebo to see if it works without side effects that are as bad or worse than the disease. The idea that smoking tobacco increases your risk of lung cancer was just a conjecture until studies were performed over a period of many years that showed a statistically higher incidence of lung cancer among those who smoked cigarettes compared with those who did not smoke, when there did not seem to be any other plausible explanation. What preceded modern science historically was the idea that you could produce truth on the conceptual level alone. Medieval theology was based in that false idea. Medieval theologians proved, on the conceptual level alone, that the sun and stars were perfect spheres that revolved around the earth in perfect circles. Galileo had the radical idea of building a telescope to actually look at what was going on and concluded that the theology was wrong. He asked the priests to look into the telescope and see for themselves. The priests refused and treated the telescope as a heretical device that could not disprove their theology. What Galileo's telescope did was to help transform the way we think. The pre-scientific idea was that concepts alone can prove the truth of concepts. The scientific idea is that concepts alone mean nothing unless they can be supported by experience. These are two radically different ways of thinking. Unfortunately, most of the way humankind thinks about politics, about ethics, about good and evil, and about religion is pre-scientific thinking. Too many people rely solely on a concept, or an idea, and are as blind as the priests in Galileo's day to experience. They won't look into the telescopes of today for fear that they will be proven wrong, or worse, that evidence is irrelevant, that facts are beside the point, and that the truth is fully contained in some document written centuries ago. All over the world, including right here in this country, humankind is in danger of having the pre-scientific mentality shove the scientific mentality aside. Then we return

Most of the way humankind thinks about politics, about ethics, about good and evil, and about religion is pre-scientific thinking. (Bob)

to Medieval times where heretics are tortured and killed. Actually, much of the world has not emerged from those pre-scientific times.

MARTIN: But Bob, where is faith in your scientific world view? I experience God through faith, but for you faith is absent, so you shut out experience of God.

BOB: Faith has no place whatsoever in my view.

HARRIET: You know, I've been thinking, maybe you two are talking about two different realms of experience. Bob, I think you are talking about the social realm, where what people agree upon requires a basis in experience. Mart, I think you are talking about a personal realm, where your relationship to God is personal between you and God, and what people agree upon in the social realm is irrelevant to that relationship. If we treat the personal realm and the social realm as two different realms of experience, then we assign science to the social realm where people need agreement to act effectively, and we assign religion to the personal realm where belief is a relationship between the believer and his beliefs that do not require agreement of others. The problem comes when we think there is only one realm of experience, that the personal realm is also the social realm, or that the social realm is also the personal realm. The social realm requires something outside of us that we can rely upon for settling disputes, and that "something outside of us" is experience that all can see, including factual studies and experiments that can be reproduced. The personal realm, on

> I experience God through faith, but for you faith is absent, so you shut out experience of God. (Martin)

the other hand, is private to each person, where what is outside of us in the world is secondary. In the personal realm, Mart can choose to believe in God and Bob can choose not to believe in God, and I can choose to believe in my weird God, but there are no facts to appeal to that can make either of us say that the other is wrong.

BOB: OK, but that would mean that there is something wrong about baseball teams sponsoring someone to sing "God Bless America" during breaks.

HARRIET: Actually that's right. It assumes, falsely, that everyone believes in God, or the same God, and should applaud this view in public. It's disrespectful of people who don't believe in God, or believe in a God that does not bless just America but all people. It turns a public sporting event into a religious affair. Totally inappropriate.

BOB: I think your point is that it disrespects individual personal beliefs by subordinating them to the social realm. It seems to me that the same thing happens on the dollar bill which says, "In God we trust." That is confusing the personal realm, where people have different views about whether there is a God or not, with the social realm of commercial transactions.

HARRIET: That too is an excellent example of the confusion I am talking about. The dollar bill is a very social entity printed by the government. It has no meaning outside of commerce, and commerce is purely a social thing that involves interaction among people and agreement as to the dollar's worth. The three of us use the dollar bill all the time

Maybe you two are talking about two different realms of experience. (Harriet)

as a medium of exchange with the rest of the world. Yet, Bob does not believe in God, and the God I trust is not the same as the God Mart trusts. So the idea of subordinating the personal realm to the social realm effectively says the personal realm does not exist, and that we all have to march in lockstep to the tune of One God in order to engage in commercial transactions. That's total nonsense.

MARTIN: Harriet, I hate to agree with you, but I think you have a point. My faith in God is my personal faith, and my faith does not require you or Bob to have the same faith. My faith is between me and God. If you don't have the same faith, that's your business and not mine. My faith is confirmed by my experience of God, but if you don't have that faith, you won't have that experience and I can't make you have it. There is no experiment or set of facts that I can appeal to, to show others that I am right. It's my own personal conviction. Still, I can join with others who have the same faith, but I cannot prove that those who don't have that faith should have it. So, really, Bob and I do not have something in common that is "outside of ourselves" to prove to Bob that I'm right about God, or for Bob to prove to me that he's right about no God, or for Harriet to prove to either of us that she's right about God. That's different from trying to show that a pill cures a disease, because we can all examine facts outside of ourselves and reach an agreement about it.

BOB: Interesting. I agree with both of you. I can see that nothing I can say will persuade Mart to stop believing in God. As long as Mart leaves me alone and doesn't call me a faithless heretic, I can leave Martin alone and not call him a delusionist. What we have to agree upon is where the personal realm leaves off and the social realm beings, and vice versa.

HARRIET: What separates the two, the personal from the social, is the presence of something outside of ourselves that all people can look at, the stuff we call evidence and facts. For example, we don't send a man off to prison just because he does not believe in God, but we do send him off to prison if we can show that he robbed a bank. We can't observe a person's beliefs. But the bank robbery is outside of us; people who saw it can describe what happened. So this event outside of us that was observable is the basis for people reaching agreement about what happened. We may get enough agreement to convict the person we think is the robber and send him off to prison. But since people make mistakes, we have to allow for that and not kill the robber or cut off his arm, but keep him around, with all of his limbs, to release if it is later determined that those who identified him were wrong, or to release when he's viewed as ready to rejoin society and not be a criminal.

BOB: Right, Harriet, because when you talk about crime, there is actually a scientific methodology that should be applied to determine guilt or innocence. The hypothesis is, "He did it." Then you look for evidence to confirm or disprove it, just as you would look for evidence to prove an hypothesis in science. The police, the lawyers, the judge and the jury are all, ideally, part of the community of inquirers that I was talking about when it comes to determining whether someone is guilty of crime.

HARRIET: And we are talking about social interactions here, since crime is a social thing that directly affects others. But I have no evidence that Mart believes in God, or that Bob doesn't, except from what you tell me and my acceptance of your statements as truthful. That's why the personal realm is different.

MARTIN: I have to admit after these discussions that I cannot prove to Bob that God exists or that he should have faith. So I have to admit that belief in God is a personal matter, not a social one. I personally am offended by seeing "In God we trust" on a dollar bill. What do you mean, "we"? I trust in God and it has nothing to do with whether anyone else does. Putting God on the dollar bill reduces God to a commercial entity and replaces faith with mass appeal.

BOB: I remember from a political science class I had that the U.S. Constitution says that there shall be no religious test for President of the United States.* I think the people who wrote that had their heads on straight. I can't say the same for the people who put God on the dollar bill.

HARRIET: Wow, you have a good memory. How many years ago was that class?

BOB: It's amazing what sticks after these years and what doesn't.

HARRIET: I wonder why it's any different when people want a President who does or does not believe in women's right to choose whether to have an abortion. It seems to me that those who believe that human life begins before birth are basing it on their religious beliefs. So to choose a candidate for President based on whether he—or maybe she some day—believes in women's right to choose, is to require a religious test for President, contrary to the Constitution.

BOB: You can say the same thing about people who think the President should believe in God, or should be a Christian,

---

* [Article VI. 3.]

or a particular kind of Christian. They are rejecting this principle contained in the Constitution. The people who wrote the Constitution were smarter than they are. Seems to me that those people recognized the point we are agreeing on, that religion and belief in God is between the individual and his or her beliefs, and that that is not a matter for social control. Politics and law refer to the social realm, and religion refers to the personal realm. I think people have lost the understanding that these two realms are quite different. Beliefs cannot be observed by others; only actions can. So that's why the First Amendment says that the government shall make no laws respecting religion.

HARRIET: And a law that says a woman can't have an abortion is a law respecting the religious beliefs of those who think abortions are against God.

MARTIN: But isn't killing a social matter, subject to laws?

HARRIET: Yes, but it's again a question of where is the line between the personal and the social. That line can't be determined by religion, or the line disappears. The line has to be determined by agreements based on observable facts that can be studied. The political and social realm ends where unprovable personal beliefs begin. The political and social begins where actions occur that affect others.

MARTIN: But an abortion is an action, and it affects others, namely the fetus.

BOB: But that begs the question. Is the fetus an "other"? We know the fetus is an other once it is born and the umbilical cord has been cut. Before that happens, there's disagreement. I'm just saying that religion and belief in God have no place in deciding what laws should be passed. Laws are a social matter.

MARTIN: But the fetus is potential life, a potential other.

HARRIET: Well, an egg inside a woman is potential human life too. Are we going to pass laws requiring women who ovulate to have sex or have sperm injected into them to protect that potential life?

BOB: I think Hitler and his followers would like that idea. To them, and unfortunately to many around the world, women only exist to bear children, preferably male children.

HARRIET: Let's not go there. It makes me sick.

BOB: I suspect religion is behind those ideas too.

MARTIN: Let's not blame religion for the world's evils. I think the idea of human equality and the golden rule have been pushed by various religions.

HARRIET: Right. I consider my views about God to be religious, and they fit perfectly with the idea of equality.

BOB: I think these ideas have been pushed by nonreligious people too. I believe in them, and I'm not religious. I believe in them not on faith but as a working hypothesis that makes sense to me given my experiences.

HARRIET: Beliefs do lead people to act in certain ways, so the personal and the social realms cannot be entirely separated, even though they are different. I view my belief in equality to be confirmed by my experience of people, but I'm not sure I would have been open to those experiences without believing that God resides within each of them and in all of them. So my beliefs do, I think, affect what experiences I give credit to.

BOB: I think it also goes the other way too. Laws can affect what people believe. The personal and the social interact. But that is not to say that laws should interfere with people's personal beliefs. So, for example, laws should not tell women whether to have an abortion or not. That's a matter of the woman's personal beliefs and not a matter for social control. But if she's inclined to kill or abuse her own born child, the laws step in and say No. The laws may actually shape what she believes and persuade her that abusing her child is wrong and clarify what is abusive and what isn't. But that does not nullify the idea that the personal and social realms are separate. The social realm consists of what can be observed, like actions, and the personal consists of what cannot be observed, like beliefs. Yes, they interact and influence one another, but they are separate.

MARTIN: I think I have to agree about them being separate. I guess if I were in the minority about believing in God and lived in a society that was mostly atheists, I'd want to assert my right to believe in God and not have the atheists pass laws against believing in God. And I'd hate it if the atheists put "There is no God" on the dollar bill. So I'm agreeing with you about the separation of the personal from the social, while realizing that they interact. It seems like preserving religion in a society full of atheists, and preserving atheism in a society full of believers, are equivalent and require laws that would allow for and protect both without favoring one over the other.

HARRIET: Well, it's good that we have reached some agreement, since tomorrow we have to leave and go to our

> The social realm consists of what can be observed, like actions, and the personal consists of what cannot be observed, like beliefs. Yes, they interact and influence one another, but they are separate. (Bob)

separate homes. This was fun. I enjoyed these discussions.

BOB: We are a weird bunch of siblings. I can't imagine anyone else having these discussions outside of a classroom. Even in a classroom, I suspect a lot of students would not actually enjoy it. But I would.

MARTIN: It's enjoyable, perhaps because we are weird, but also because our classroom consisted of the beautiful park, the congenial coffee shop, and this comfortable living room where we can sip cordials—and there are no final exams and no grades.

HARRIET: Yes, that's a pleasant note on which to end. We can think about these things without having exams hanging over our heads. I'm sure we will have more to talk about when we get together again.

BOB: Well there is one thing we should think about. How do we get others to be more respectful of non-traditional believers and especially of nonbelievers?

MARTIN: In a democratic society, such respect should be the norm.

THE AUTHOR

John L. Hodge has published writings about democracy, ethics, culture and law. He recently published a book, *How We Are Our Enemy—And How to Stop: Our Unfinished Task of Fulfilling the Values of Democracy* (2011). He also publishes online his blog on democracy, human rights and ethical values: JohnLHodge.blogspot.com. He is the main co-author of *Cultural Bases of Racism and Group Oppression: An Examination of Traditional "Western" Concepts, Values and Institutional Structures Which Support Racism, Sexism and Elitism* (1975). He also wrote "Democracy and Free Speech: A Normative Theory of Society and Government," Chapter 5 of *The First Amendment Reconsidered* (1982); and "Equality: Beyond Dualism and Oppression," Chapter 6 of *Anatomy of Racism* (1990). At Yale University in the 1960's he wrote his Ph.D. dissertation that proposed a philosophical, nonreligious basis for a form of pacifism that allows for self-defense. In addition to his writings, his work includes practical endeavors that supported his view of a democratic society. In the 1960's he was a draft counselor and peace intern with the American Friends Service Committee in Houston and Seattle. As a college teacher and university professor from 1968-1979, he taught courses addressing racism, sexism, the Vietnam war, and other ethical, social and political issues, mostly at California State University, East Bay. While teaching there, he was a member and chair of the Affirmative Action Committee of a statewide faculty union. After receiving his law degree in 1980, and after serving as Law Clerk for the Massachusetts Appeals Court and Staff Attorney for the U. S. Court of Appeals for the First Circuit, he worked primarily for Massachusetts state agencies that provided health care, such as Medicaid. He directly participated in the successful efforts of these agencies that greatly expanded health care coverage and provided a model for national health care. He has an A.B. in mathematics from the University of Kansas (where he graduated as a member of Phi Beta Kappa), a Ph.D. in philosophy from Yale University, and a law degree (J.D.) from the University of California, Berkeley (Boalt Hall). He lives with his wife in the Boston area.

www.ingramcontent.com/pod-product-compliance
Lightning Source LLC
Chambersburg PA
CBHW021207020426
42331CB00003B/244